15 MANTRAS FOR EFFECTIVE COMMUNICATION

ACHIEVE SUCCESS @ WORKPLACE

MOHITA DATTA

ISBN 979-888555198-4

Dedicated to the Muse of Communication

I seek her in inspiration, thinking situations, reworking conversations, juggling thoughts, reading, writing... almost in every waking moment.

And sometimes she jilts me when I need her the most. And I know it's time to rewrite, reframe moments, and work ahead. She visits me often.

Love and dedication to my Muse, you keep me inspired!

Contents

Contents

Foreword

Written by Paul A. Argenti, Professor of Corporate Communication, The Tuck School of Business at Dartmouth, USA

"*Having worked on a book project over a decade ago with Mohita Datta, I already was aware of her incredible talents as a researcher and the depth of her knowledge as a communicator. Now, I see that she is also capable of writing a significant study of communication. In this book, she has written an extremely effective step-by-step guide for anyone interested in honing their written and oral communication skills. Each chapter is a building block toward making yourself a more effective communicator. Her examples are simple, the characters she writes about are based on real people, and her writing style is very accessible.*

hat particularly grabbed my attention in this book was the idea of associating mantras with effective communication. A mantra is often said to be a thought or seed for energizing intention. Her 15 seeds, focused on everything from the most basic questions of communication to erasing mental blocks, and mastering the art of persuasion, can lead to some incredibly powerful intentions for those seeking guidance about their communications.

Mohita also uses some great quotes to make her points. One that caught my eye was this from Woody Allen ~ If all my possessions were taken from me with one exception, I would hope to keep my power of communication for by it I would regain all the rest.

And another from Maya Angelou to make a point about the power of the human voice ~ Words mean more than what is set down on paper. It takes the human voice to infuse them with deeper meaning ~ Indeed.

So, no matter what you are looking for in terms of communications associated with your job, your home life, your parenting, this book has something for you: ***How can you make a good first impression? How do you research your topic? How do you organize your speech for success? Each chapter, or mantra as she calls them, offers us the opportunity to plant the seed for energizing our intention and getting to the next level.***

After 40 years of researching, teaching, and consulting about corporate communication, Mohita Datta's book made me realize we all need to get back to the fundamentals of communication to be good at our jobs no matter what we do. If you are looking for a comprehensive guidebook on how to communicate, or you are looking to review the basics of communication, this easy to access book is for you."

Paul Argenti is a pioneer in the field of corporate communication, teaching the earliest courses on the subject for Harvard Business School, Columbia Business School, and the Tuck School of Business at Dartmouth. Books he has authored include: Corporate

Communication, Corporate Responsibility, Digital Strategies for Powerful Corporate Communication, The Power of Corporate Communication, and has actively contributed insightful articles in Harvard Business Review, New York, Wall Street Journal, Washington Post

Written by Sreemoyee Piu Kundu, acclaimed journalist and columnist

> *"Communication is key to navigating the modern world and noone shows us better than specialist Mohita Datta who brings to her debut novel, not just an astute understanding of the paradigm of what it means to be a communication pro - but why the language and interactivity of communication is integral to interpersonal and professional relationships.* ***Crisply written with chapters that are both practical and immersive - Datta is one of the voices you don't want to miss. I would highly recommend this book in media schools, PR and Marcomm agencies and also as an individual must read."***

Sreemoyee Piu Kundu, bestselling author: Status Single, Sita's Curse, Cut!. Columnist on sexuality and gender and community founder of SWIFT (Single Women of India Forward Together), **India's first and only community for urban single women. Organising the first ever Summit on single women in India, writing columns on women & gender, curating Women's Festivals, D&I conferences & live talk shows.**

Written by Sweta Samota, acclaimed Book Coach, Best-selling Author, and Changemaker

"When I met Mohita in a Changemakers event, I instantly connected with her. What grabbed my attention was the way she communicated with me and everyone else at the event! And what touched my heart is her genuineness, humility and love for her work. The qualities of a great communicator! Mohita is one of the best trainers in her field and when she decided to write a book, I knew it would be one of the "must" handbooks for every individual. She has been a Corporate Trainer for several years. So, it's a treat to get all the practical tips in this handbook. I particularly like that she has covered both the basics as well as the advanced topics like non-verbal communication, visual aids and the art of persuasion.

You know the secret to success? One of the key things to master? One of them is communication. Grab the book and get started on your journey to become a Master Communicator and a successful individual. "

Sweta Samota also dons on the role of being a Motivational Speaker and influencer, with elan. Her bestselling books include: Nine, Radha in a Jinx, Kiss of True Love, The 5 Secrets of Highly Successful Authors, Changemakers: 11 Change Stories from Inspiring Indian Women. An intrepid writer, and writer-mentor, with a calling for spiritual, she lives by the vision: "*Be the Change you wish to see in the world.'"*- ***Mahatma Gandhi***

FOREWORD

Preface

What if you could master persuasion, boost career growth, and build a roadmap to success? What if you had the magical mantras to open doors of opportunity?

Life is a series of crucial situations and communications: whether it is preparing for an important job interview, or practicing to deliver a new presentation, or introducing yourself at a networking event, or making small talk at a party, so many situations and the one skill you need the most is **Communications**.

Here's a handy book to build up your communication skills step-by-step, in such a way that you remember and use them in your everyday life.

Learn the art and science of Effective Communication! These 15 mantras will ensure that you have an edge in the outcome of crucial situations.

This book will make you an effective communicator! And that's a promise.

Acknowledgements

The book is finally here. I always thought I'll be writing one but wasn't too sure on which topic and when. And then I chose a theme closest to my heart and mind: Communications. I think an ocean dwells there. Wherever you dive, you will come out with a beautiful treasure or a treatise, as you want it.

Also, this has been my Karma-Bhoomi, and something I identify with closely. My post-graduate qualifications and work experience all pointed this way. My work and play all dwelt here. Communications is what was to be; an area whose far corners I have been able to explore, and where the jigsaw puzzle pieces fall into place as soon as I look at them. That's the magic. It's the coming together of a curious mind and conscious living.

This book has had a smooth journey that may not have been possible without peace and joy at home; the credit for keeping our home front equitable and tranquil goes to my husband **Raakesh Datta**. I now understand there is something called silent support that is very giving and unquestioning. Thank you, Raakesh.

And then I got waves of charged energy from folks I knew I could count on, and cheering friends and mentors. On top of the list please find **Sweta Samota**, her positive and purposive energy was such a boost. Also, she knew where the headwind and drag factors were coming from and would nudge me whenever I lost speed. Sweta was my accountability partner too, and she went beyond the brief. I share the achievement of having brought out the book with her.

Arjun needed Krishna to cut through the babble of noises clouding the mind and to lay the strategy in the battlefield homing into the target. And I needed my own army of mentors and strategists.

My list of acknowledgments has an eminent place for my sister **Rajita Majumdar** who has been my joyful support in life and for this venture, also a dedicated sounding-board. Being a Communications person too, she helped by giving valuable insights, and a third-party pro-preview. We have many journeys planned together going ahead, and the greatest enjoyment comes from having travel buddies.

It has been a long journey, but not how the word 'long' sounds; it has not been arduous or backbreaking or steeped in struggles type of journey, but 'seeking-wise' long for I took many detours into coves of learnings along the way.

And now begins the roll of honor with my friend and associate **Geetika Singh** spearheading it. She has been there in every little step - bouncing off ideas, keeping the milestones together, adding new skills, extending our horizons. It's wonderful how the universe gives you companions without you expecting any.

My edit and critique credit go to **Niladri Mitra** and **Vatsala Kaul**. Niladri besides being the official editor of the book has added value to it by his constant suggestions of adding visibility to the treatise. Vatsala has been the push and prompt behind the scenes, and having decades of experience in the publishing industry her suggestions were most valuable and experiential. Thank you, Vatsala.

Tanya Kumar, a talented architect, and teacher of structural dynamics has been my trusted go-to source for infinite creative and visual tinkering. Before-the-dawn breaks type of a friend are few and far between and she's one of them. I have had all my fronts covered with late-night friends too; I count upon **Sreemoyee Piu Kundu**, strength for single women and a reputed columnist on gender and sexuality, as my ally, lighting up the alleyways. What amazes me, and makes me happy is that all my friends and allies showed such resonance with bringing out my book, and were party to all my journeys as an author.

My school friends, my college and hostel pals, my Mass Communication buddies echoed enthusiasm for my author venture and were there for me. **Shalini Modi** rose to the occasion and hosted a Book Reading event for me amongst pals, and I would like to think that we raised the levels of awareness for Communications as a single most important skill to enhance life experiences and calibrate the outcome. **Rohit**, her husband, and Shalini cheered and celebrated the launch of my book, and these moments make you believe that there's more than celebrating birthdays and anniversaries.

Life is a crucible and it gives you so many golden opportunities to reinvent yourself. You just have to keep the doors and windows of yourself open to the fresh zephyr.

My school friend **Neeraj** stole the march in pouring with enthusiasm about stacks of books waiting to be written. She reiterated that this is just the beginning, a learning experience, and I must now plan with more writings. I love these cheerleaders of mine! And then there are more in my arsenal waiting to be counted, let's begin with **Vinita and her wonderful husband Sunny, Chhabi, Shilpi, and Harmeen**, and then the list is endless. I never thought my schoolmates will be there for me, forever. Thanks a lot, my friends! Gratitude is a word I knew early on but understood the meaning only in recent times.

My mentor, relative, and friend are all rolled into one person **Dr. Priya Sharma**, and all my ventures are complete once she congratulates and celebrates. Thanks a lot, Priya for being intrinsic support in my life, and all its adventures. And the roll-of-honur has an important inclusion: my mother-in-law **Dr Krishna Datta**, her perserverence to all interests educational kept the literary fire burning.

And then folks ask where do I get my never-say-die spirit! Or the art of staying relevant and alive, pushing all the fronts and the answer should surprise none ... the credit goes to my early influencer, my mother, **Indu Bhatnagar**. She can look at every trouble in the eye, and carry on having given spin to the situation.

> ***"The one person I miss in this journey is my father, he made sure early on that we had secure personalities, and celebrated our small wins, and let nothing in the world deter us from having faith in ourselves. Such implicit trust makes me perennially a happy person."***

I do have a critic at home, and that should be rephrased to a person offering critique, and the honor goes to my daughter **Arushi Datta**. Her economy with words is helpful and focused, and carries gravitas so needed when you need to chisel your product to a definite shape and purpose. She has been my lens through which I look at the emerging trends and a touchstone for my ideologies, and correctness.

I need to write a note of appreciation to so many people who have offered me dynamic opportunities and platforms to grow; I would like to include **Avani Bhatnagar**, the magnetic leader in Corporate Training, **Dimple Ahuja**, my teacher and master practitioner for NLP, **Smriti Sood**, mentor and energizer for all things under Learning and Development.

Also, I deeply appreciate the experiential insights of my niece **Tanvi Majumdar** who's been my partner in exploring new features of social media platforms, and together we decoded what's the best way to go about it.

And here's a forget-me-not note for my SCM pals .... **Rani Chandok, Sumita Hattangadi, Lorella Jacinto, Anuradha Naggarkate**!! The most beautiful and formative years of my life were formed in Bomaby, aka Mumbai, where we eager-beaver students of SCM (Social Communication Media) enthusistically followed every lecture and practical at Sophia College. Yen for learning all things intrinsic to communication took roots then. It has been an abiding love story since then.

And I would like to close the roll of honor with **Prof Paul A. Argenti, Tuck School of Business, Dartmouth, USA** who ignited the passion for communication and writing on it, and seeded my intent on going that way. Million thanks for being there in my constellation of stars sparkling light and direction! When I collated research and writing for his book Strategic Corporate Communications, a decade back, I had no idea that I would be impassioned to take the same path. I am deeply honored that he has given a glowing recommendation for my book, and it remains my biggest motivation to lift the bar higher, in coming times.

Sweta tells me that we are all spiritual in a way, perhaps it's true, and I do think that there were mellifluous and euphonic notes in my ear as I wrote this treatise for everyone.

Dear friends and associates, thank you for being there, for me.

Prologue

"And then there was this conversation which changed my life"

Oh really! When did it happen? Or are you just imagining it? Has this detailed script of dialog-by-dialog rally really taken place, or do you wish it had?

Yes, these life-changing conversations are what dreams are made of: perfect, polished, expressive, with rich outcomes. In reality, when we wake up from such beautiful dreams and have to face the critical situation, our conversation seems to have a life of its own: it careens, veers off course and goes downhill, very often. You have not been able to convey your point of view. What could have been an opportunity to change the dynamics of an equation, express yourself clearly and reap rich rewards, ends up with no consequence. Or worse still gets you into conflict course.

Take time to understand the dynamics of communication, and how to build on this critical skill. People I interviewed for the book: economists, management thoroughbreds, entrepreneurs and venture capitalists all profess the same thing: In this age of robotic working, artificial intelligence, globalization, automation — the one skill that can separate you not only from the technology that we create but from your peers is mastering the ancient art of communication and persuasion. Combining words and ideas to ignite people's imagination.

I have field-tested my entire course and those who have benefited from these techniques include business clients generating millions in additional profits, MBA students getting better jobs, and even parents dealing with their children. The book shows you how to use these skills in the workplace and in every other realm of your life.

It's also eminently practical. In these pages, you will find the techniques for getting the deal you want.

Try it out for yourself, you will be surprised at how effective it is. Just be prepared to put in the work required to learn a new skill.

> "*Winston Churchill said, "The difference between mere management and leadership is communication."*"

Epigraph

"Communication is your ticket to success, if you pay attention and learn to do it effectively."

~ Theo Gold

CHAPTER ONE

Communication: Ladder to Success

- Beginning with the strange case of Shreya Sharma
- Understanding an Effective Communication Cycle
- Good Communication Leads the Way. Bad Communication Spoils the Day

Communication: Ladder to Success

"Communication works for those who work at it." ~John Powell

Beginning with the strange case of Shreya Sharma

Who is to blame? *Communication Imbroglio*

Shreya, 31 years old, armed with a doctorate degree in Public Health & Management Policy from an esteemed university in UK, was on a job-hunt at her home ground in Delhi when she encountered a rather perplexing situation. She was called for an interview which did not happen as per the expected plan. She was proud of her academic achievements and labor of more than a decade in higher learning and research. A close friend had passed on a reference for a suitable opening at Juniper India. Shreya was excited with the profile of both the job and the organization. She soon heard from the HR of the organization and her online Zoom interview was confirmed for the upcoming Saturday.

At the due hour, Shreya logged into the Zoom link. She rearranged her doctorate papers, certificates, and other credentials, on her work desk. Soon the screen came alive and she was happy to note that she looked neat and professional with her hair pinned back and wearing her favorite black silk attire. She was ready to face Sharmishta Sen, Director - Public Policy & Analytics. Shreya had already browsed through an important lecture series by Ms. Sen in preparation; who had been marked in all the mails, as the person who would be conducting the interview. But to her surprise, a much younger guy named Pranav appeared on the screen. His designation placard did not relate to the department she had applied to. He was neither from the HR department nor did he look like a high ranking official. At best he seemed to be a junior executive. *What was happening? Hope he was not going to be the sole interviewer. Will he tell her that he was just filling in for Ms. Sen who was a bit late for the interview? Or that this online interaction was going to be followed up with another add-on interview with the higher management? Should they not have rescheduled the interview in such a case?* However, none of that happened.

Pranav asked her some routine questions and Shreya answered in a haze. Nothing incisive, no talk about her Doctorate papers, no questions about her specialization, or when could she join the organization. It all ended too soon. The next thing she knew he had ended the zoom call with some uninspiring '*Good Day*' phrase.

For the next couple of days, Shreya was a mix of emotions - heartbroken, bitter, resentful, frustrated at being treated in such a cavalier fashion; and perplexed at what could have possibly brought this strange descent of happenings. *Why didn't the organization inform her earlier about the change of interviewer? Why was this junior, obviously inexperienced, and definitely not qualified in her field of knowledge, assigned to be her interviewer? Was the organization even going to follow it up?* She had pinned her hopes on Juniper Org. This was one company which suited her work profile best and could offer her a good growth path. Her listless countenance worried her parents. They hoped to lift her out of her low spirits and demotivated state by encouraging her to write to the company about her poor experience. But she had struck a mental resistance and could not bring herself to write to Ms. Sen and others at Juniper.

Now this is a classic case of poor communication, miscommunication, and missed opportunities for effective communication. A situation that could have been mutually beneficial for all involved ended up being a losing proposition for everyone. Let us explore every stakeholder's cases and see what could have happened, had conscious and responsible communication taken place.

What people could have done differently to achieve the objective of Effective Communication and Positive Outcome:

Ms. Sen - ***Director Public Policy & Analytics, Juniper Org:***

- Written to Shreya apologizing for her absence, assuring her that the person deputed for taking her interview will follow up the case diligently, and report back to her
- Posted a feedback after the interview, and looped in Shreya as to when could she expect a reply from Juniper Org

Pranav - ***The Interviewer from Juniper Org:***

- Should have updated Shreya about Ms. Sen's absence, if not already done; and assured her that he would be taking over responsible charge in the meantime
- Posted her a message after the interview informing her of timeline for the decision-making process, or any next steps required from her end
- Being responsible and pro-active are the true qualities of an effective communicator

Shreya Sharma -*The Aspirant:*

- After the initial disappointment, and that sinking feeling, she should have rebooted her inner resources, cleared up her head, taken a deep breath and acknowledged the change of interviewer
- Be mindful of whoever is sitting across you; you never know the powers the person wields
- Shreya should have politely enquired if Ms. Sen would not be there for the interview, giving Pranav a chance to clarify, and also to reset her own mind for the interview ahead
- Asked at the end of the interview as to when would she be hearing from them, and if she needs to do anything next. Be proactive
- After not having heard from the organization for a week, followed up with an email to the HR head as to what was in store for her, also stating that she missed Ms. Sen for the critical interview
- Further followed it up with a call to the necessary officials, if required

The situation above is a major loss for everyone.

The company lost an opportunity to establish its brand credibility on a young qualified aspirant. Juniper is a communications organization in disseminating global health policies. For a communications company it majorly bungled up its own communication. They came away looking as a heavy-handed archaic organization with no responsible attitude towards young talented people seeking to join the workplace. That is an important stakeholder's category. Also in the contemporary era, word travels fast. This incident could hurt the company's ability to attract qualified talent with its random and clumsy communication or rather lack of it. The company definitely lost on all counts of communication with its poor communication, miscommunication and missed opportunities for communication.

The Organization - ***Juniper Org lost on count of poor communication:***

- Loss of brand value
- Poor perception amongst its stake holders
- Lost out on promising talent
- Loss of a certain growth path

The Aspirant -***Shreya Sharma lost on count of missed opportunity for purposive communication:***

- Missed acknowledging and accepting the substitute/ new interviewer
- Missed reframing her answers for the benefit of the new interviewer, whose baseline of understanding may not have been that of Ms. Sen, the head of the department
- Missed checking for feedback - whether the new interviewer was following her responses or if he needed

any clarifications

- Missed giving quality responses to the questions asked
- Missed giving her best shot in the new situation
- Missed following up the interview with email/s which could have influenced the outcome as showing her to be an interested and enthusiastic candidate
- Missed the opportunity to put it on record that the original interviewer was not present
- Missed the mega-opportunity to let the management know she still has good perception of the organization and is interested in knowing the outcome

Different communication strategies have different outcomes. Not all can be calculated to a decimal place. But having no communication strategy can only result in no progress. A blank slate deserves no comment.

"Good communication is the bridge between confusion and clarity."

~ Nat Turner

When reading the above situation, many of us would think *Yes, this seems to be the natural way of addressing or correcting the situation.* But how many of us would really apply this to the situation? How often do we pro-actively draft a communication strategy and benefit ourselves? And coincidentally benefitting others too. As we know, good communication benefits both the sender and the receiver. It really delivers you from darkness to light. No kidding! You will discover in the chapters ahead that mindful communication brings you closer to your set objective. You start with understanding effective communication, and tools to improve it, and you end up being a better YOU, both in a professional and personal space.

More often than not we are stuck in a morass of poor communication with poor outcomes, and give in to early frustration and criticism. And that's largely unproductive. Unfortunately, we realize it too but face inertia in extricating ourselves from our present predicament. It's time to say hello to the *Shakti* or Superpower called Effective Communication!

Here is an opportunity to decode practices and principles of effective communication, to understand what makes a person tick in simple to tough situations, and to make progress in life.

Effective communication is applied communication, where you are conscious of the choices you are making, and are alert to the outcomes. Simply speaking, you are here to achieve your goals through communication.

Think about your workplace where time is limited and opportunities are numbered. It makes double the sense to understand the tenets of effective communication and practice them regularly. In addition to your skills, understanding the tenets of effective communication and their regular practice will boost your career prospects. You don't have the luxury of going over and over again in an unplanned fashion, where each day is paid for and you are supposed to deliver outcomes. Use the opportunities and your time there to reap rich rewards. Your field knowledge combined with effective communication is your **Brahmastra*.

Don't miss the target. Equip yourself with tools of effective communication.

**Brahmastra*: *Powerful and celestial weapons used during the mythological war of Mahabharata*

Understanding an Effective Communication Cycle

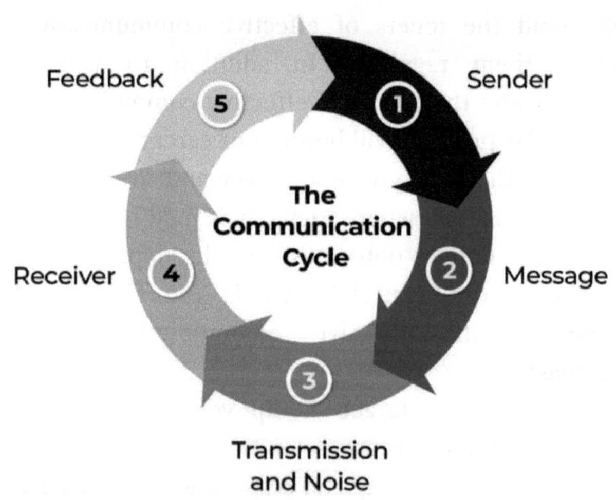

COMMUNICATION CYCLE

We can now relate to an Effective Communication Cycle:We communicate each and every day, almost every minute of our waking lives. It is something intrinsic to us. Wouldn't it be wonderful if this essential part of us is shaped, forged, and fine-tuned to serve our interests better!

Let us disseminate the cycle into its most basic elements.

Sender:

The person who communicates the message is the sender. The sender has the responsibility to encode the message clearly and succinctly. For effective communication to happen it is imperative that the sender understands:

- The target audience who has to receive the message
- And the purpose of the message

Message:

This is information, or knowledge, that the sender wishes to communicate to the receiver. Sender can choose any channel of communication - verbal, non-verbal or written - which suits their purpose. This is further customized as per sender's style of communication, choice of words, actions and time, also tonality, and presentation.

For effective communication to take place, the message should be:

- Clearly expressed as per understanding of the receiver/ target audience
- Encoded correctly for Call to action, if any

Transmission and Noise:

The transmission of the message is the actual process of sending it. This could be done via various verbal and written communication channels. For example - email, letters, texts, reports, face-to-face, telephone and videoconferencing.

Noise is a bunch of all the factors which can become barriers to transmitting the sender's message. And this noise can obfuscate the message, making it liable to being misunderstood by the target audience, or not producing the desired result.

Noise may be physical - like the phone line not being clear or internet connectivity being poor for video conferencing; or noise could be psychological - for example if the audience is biased or judgmental or having assumptions while receiving the message; or the noise could be semantic - meaning the challenge here pertains to language, where jargon, or accent, or language itself, is the roadblock to being understood.

For effective communication to take place, the sender has to ensure:

- The message is clear and without noise; anticipate eruption of noise if any, and encode the message accordingly
- Transmission and channels of transmission are free of problems; test the channels before important communication has to take place

Receiver:

Simply speaking receiver is the one who receives the message and interprets it by decoding its components - words, graphics, audios, visual props, etc. If the message is received with the same meaning and context as the sender wants to convey, we can safely say that effective communication has taken place.

In this case for effective communication to take place, the receiver must:

- Also ensure that the channels of receiving are clear, and noise-free; with no biases and prejudices coloring the intended message
- Co-operate with the sender to respond with clear signals of understanding

Feedback:

The most critical element of any communication is Feedback. This communicates to the sender that the receiver has understood the message clearly and there is no scope for misunderstanding.

For effective communication to take place:

- Timely feedback must be collected from the audience which can be verbal or non-verbal
- Message must be adjusted as per the feedback

Good Communication Leads the Way; Bad Communication Spoils the Day

Here's a telling example. A Manager needs to tell his team that the company is undergoing change and if they want to hold onto their positions, they need to reskill. But because of his garbled unplanned communication, the message gives rise to resentment and anxiety amongst the team members. The big fallout is unproductivity and office politics. This negative and toxic occurrence could have been handled adroitly with:

- In-person and collective communication about company's plans ahead
- Addressing the concerns and giving a career growth-path ahead
- Handling feedback if any

The Manager unfortunately did not plan his communication strategy well, neither did he apply himself to the situation to mitigate the noise factor nor did he choose the transmission channel mindfully; and it resulted in an enormous swell of dissatisfaction amongst the employees.

In case of unsuccessful transmission there is a breakdown of relationships and communication. While in case of successful transmission the ideas and thoughts are the same as conveyed by the sender to the receiver, resulting in productivity and trust.

The first quality of a visionary leader is good communication.

> ***"Communication is a skill that you can learn. It's like riding a bicycle or typing. If you're willing to work at it, you can rapidly improve the quality of every part of your life."***

~ Brian Tracy

CHAPTER TWO

The Why, What, How of Communication; Answers to Your Everyday Questions

- Why communicate?
- What do we mean by "communication"?
- What is the difference between talking and communicating?
- Why is it called a skill?
- Why is it called a "critical skill"?
- Can it be self-taught?
- Is it liberating or limiting?

The Why, What, How of Communication; Answers to Your Everyday Questions

I KEEP six honest serving-men
(They taught me all I knew);
Their names are What and Why and When
And How and Where and Who.
I send them over land and sea,
I send them east and west;
But after they have worked for me,
I give them all a rest.

Rudyard Kipling

Poets, communicators, leaders, managers, orators, mentors, entrepreneurs - all have mastery over one skill: Communication. Some common questions lead us to some uncommon answers and unique positions on Communication and how to work at it to become a powerful and good Communicator.

Why Communicate?

To be able to transfer your thoughts, ideas, information to the other person is an essential life skill. To understand others and be understood. We communicate for a variety of reasons - to give information, to answer, to comment, to establish bond, to give feedback, to foster relationships, to assess, to prompt social conversations. There can be infinite reasons. Without communication we will be islands of existence with no channels to holistic progress.

To be a Good Communicator: You will use the tool of Communication to "effectively" and "efficiently" transfer ideas. Also with tools of communication, we influence changes to our and other people's attitudes and actions, help ourselves and the person take the next step. Keep everyone motivated.

What do we mean by Communication?

Communication is transferring information from at least one person to another person or group. It involves three critical elements - the sender, the recipient, and the message. For communication to happen, the message must travel through any channel of communication and be received by the recipient. The channels of communication may include phone calls, video conferencing, emails, face-to-face conversation, written letters and memos, messaging and formal proposals, audio-conferencing.

To be a Good Communicator: You will watch out for context, culture, emotional wellbeing, mutually understood language, to ensure that the message is received with the same relevance and impact, as intended. So ideally the message sent by the sender should mean exactly the same to the recipient. The responsibility rests on the sender to be able to encode words, thoughts, emotions, impressions, needs, information in a way that it is effectively consumed by the receiver.

> "*Effective communication is that which contains the truth, which is beneficial to the listener, pleasant to hear and which is made only after self study.*"

~ Bhagvad Gita

What is the difference between Talking and Communicating?

Transition from being a mindless talker to an Effective Communicator:

Talking is simply uttering of words, intending to get a message across. It's a hit or miss action. Communication on the other hand is many steps ahead - as it ensures that the message gets transmitted successfully. It's a skill worth learning and excelling at.

To be a Good Communicator: You must learn how to transform your thoughts and actions from auto-pilot mode to a strategized one using important tools of communication. Then you will transit from being a mindless talker to an effective communicator.

You will be able to relay your best thoughts, ideas, skills, and inputs efficiently without loss of transmission and also be able to grasp the responses to them. With this complete cycle of talking and listening, you will be mindfully equipped to take action ahead and move nearer to your objective. There is no great leader who is not a great communicator.

Why do we still pepper our essays, our motivational talks, with quotes from Gandhi or Swami Vivekananda or Field Marshall Manekshaw or Subhash Chandra Bose or Winston Churchill? Because undoubtedly, besides being great leaders, they were also phenomenal orators!

Why is it called a skill?

"A ***skill*** *is the learned* ***ability*** *to perform an action with an objective in mind in a given amount of time or energy, or both.* ***Skills*** *can often be divided into domain-general and domain-*

specific **skills."**

So Communication is a learned skill and if applied mindfully and consciously, then it takes you nearer to your objective. Random and directionless talking just fills up time, but not the mind. It neither helps the talker/sender nor the listener/receiver to go to next step, or actualize action.

Communication straddles both domains - general, as it's used in day-to-day informal speaking, and also domain-specific when used as a tool or an arrow to hit the target, and achieve the objective. This is most pronounced at workplaces as it is structured for goals and bottom lines.

To be a Good Communicator: You will use the ability of effective communication for transmitting and receiving information. Using them on everyday basis, good communication skills will empower you to communicate clearly, effectively and efficiently. We learn this skill and hone it with practice, to achieve our objective at workplace and in other social contexts.

Why is it called a "critical skill"?

Communication is a critical and strategic skill which is very important for workplace success. In fact, it cannot be called just a soft skill - as it can make or break a deal. So to be competent in life, business, and leadership, you need to excel at mindful communication.

To be a good communicator, your communication skills at workplace must - boost productivity, enhance positivity, and enable competencies for yourself and others. Communication is the best way to create strong relationships.

Can it be self-taught?

Yes, you can educate yourself on principles of good and effective communication; imbue them, practice them, and seek feedback to check your progress on this critical skill. Begin with taking an assessment test on your communication proficiency, underline the parameters which need improvement, and mindfully apply the given tools to your everyday communication to improve on those chosen points.

To be a good communicator: You may find it helpful to adopt an action-based technique called **Start, Continue andStop**. This is especially useful post-feedback as you can **Start** a few new things, **Continue** a few things you find you are doing well on, and **Stop** some which you find are obstructing effective communication. Combining such focused techniques with mindful application will definitely make you a better and quick learner, and a practitioner of effective communication skills.

Is it liberating or limiting?

Communication is a discipline of knowledge which liberates you. Once you understand and master the skill set required for effective communication; you will know which all tools can work in a given situation, and apply them accordingly. A continued practice of good communication skills can bring you to a point where you can get the outcome you desire in a particular situation. Therefore, they say the route to success at workplace and life lies through communication. And that is liberating for sure because you are connecting with people on real ground and are aligning your purpose and agenda on a common plane.

To be a good communicator: You must know that communication is a fine fusion of both Science and Art. As with Science - Communication is a body of knowledge complete with laws, theory, and facts. It is also an Art - as the personalized application and creativeness will demonstrate its ultimate success in a particular situation. They say communication works for those, who work at it.

It is liberating as you know that some sort of communication will definitely work in the most disastrous or complex situations, provided you understand it. Successful people know how to communicate for results. And the collateral benefits are inclusivity, innovation, clarity, purpose, and fun.

Good communication leads to greater personal growth and empowerment. It makes for a stronger leader, a more productive team player, and a more effective person.

What are Affirmations? How do they help??

Affirmations are positive statements which motivate us. They boost mind-body-health and help us set our goals; they also bring in changes to our habits, patterns, and thoughts.

We repeat these to ourselves until we accept them into our subconscious thoughts and beliefs. Repetition is important, and allows the affirmations to sink into the subconscious mind; and bring positive changes into our lives.

Believe in the power of positive affirmations.
We are what we communicate.

Affirmation For Today That'll Change The Way You Think

"The more positive I am, the easier it is for me to have conversations and communications"

CHAPTER THREE

GET TO THE POINT!

- Learn these 3 Cs of Communication: Clear, Concise, Consistent
- Keep It Short and Simple! KISS principle

Short Stories for You: Send it like Arushi!

Get to the Point!

"Make sure to communicate your idea quickly and keep it straight to the point."

~Paul Bailey

Learn these 3 Cs of Communication: Clear, Concise, Consistent

Clear: Be clear. Be understood in the context and intent you wanted. If you need to refine your purpose; do not hesitate, it will save everyone a lot of time.

Concise: Communicate to the point. Keep your message brief, so that scope of misunderstanding does not exist. Literally.

Consistent: Nobody appreciates consistency more than your manager, client, peers, and vendor - anybody you are dealing with externally or internally for purpose of action. So please be consistent in your ***ask***. If you want change in the course of action or purpose, communicate clearly stating the reason.

There is no shortcut to being a perfect communicator. But the three Cs definitely help you get closer to your goal of achieving it.

Keep It Short and Simple: KISS Principle

Your ***ask***, the purpose behind it, and communication leading to it should be short. Don't get lost in the labyrinth of circuitous communication leading to nothing. Break down your goals into shorter ***asks***. People are wary of big changes, and the results which flow from them. Break it down into manageable chunks which look possible and promising. *KISS your Goals!! You are nearing there.*

Short Stories for You: Send it like Arushi!

What happens when you are in a high pressure job with unrealistic deadlines and extra competitive work atmosphere - which is results driven and has people with different communication styles? A perfect recipe for stress and miscommunication, until you are extra-careful. To stay productive and mitigate stress may be a tough task here, until done with strategy and goals.

Arushi realizes it as she works at a high-energy start-up, and she has developed her own practices of good communication to tackle tension-producing situations. Whenever unsettling emails land in her inbox, she takes time to frame a reply and never hits the SEND button in a hurry. It may take hours or sometimes even a day - as she would come back to the mail, reassess the contents of the mail, readjust her outlook and perspective, check for clarity and tonality in her reply, draw attention to some points if needed... only when she's sure that she has worded it just right, and will be construed so, that is when she lets it go.

"Three things that never come back; the spent arrow, the spoken word and the lost opportunity. "

~William Gregory Paige.

"I am honest and forthright in all business communications"

MOHITA DATTA

CHAPTER FOUR

Erase the Mental Blocks

- But I don't have time!
- I'm doing fine!
- Why should I care about people's understanding!
- It's not my job!
- What do I have to gain!

Short Stories for You: The Boss Has Changed!

Erase the Mental blocks

"Don't let mental blocks control you. Set yourself free. Confront your fear and turn the mental blocks into building blocks."

~ Dr. Roopleen

But I don't have time!

"Hey! Just sending this important info, I really don't have time to frame it right!"
"I don't have time to waste on soft skills like communication; I've got important things to do."
"My qualifications work for me; not COMMUNICATION!!"

If this has been your line of thinking, then you obviously got it all wrong here! If you do not use the tenets of communication in the prescribed situation, it will land you in disaster. Not the outcome you were looking for.

Let us take an example of incomplete communication: Your boss entrusted you with the file of Future Projects; to share it with relevant team members, call a meeting to discuss it, and take it forward. However, you short changed by giving incomplete information ahead.

You thought your work pressure exempted you from following good communication practices, and you could bring in quick decisions. Consequently, you did not call or write to your deputy regarding the sensitivity of the information coming their way. You did not call or write to them. You did not attach a note to the Future Projects file alerting them of how critical it is. You also did not let the other team members know that, after your deputy had added their own notes to it, the file would be coming to them.

The consequences are not tough to guess. Your deputy spilled the critical information on Future Projects, as per their understanding of need to share. Soon, there was an environment of gossip and misconstruing of facts. It went to the extent that some workers became hostile assuming that Future Projects had no place for them.

Outcome of this half-baked communication is mistrust, waste of time, waste of energy, loss of direction, and now the need was of severe damage-control measures to stop the information from possibly going viral.

Serious losses:

- Loss of trust by your boss as to how you handle information and communication
- Loss of trust by your Deputy for making them the scapegoat; while giving timely and complete information could have saved the day
- Loss of trust by your team members as to the intent of your plans

Complete communication would have saved you time and frustrations. And it would definitely have ensured progress on your career path.

I'm doing fine!

"I have aced my subjects, my knowledge domain is unbeatable, what is the necessity of learning good principles of communication?" As an IT engineer or someone with similar technical qualifications, it may lead you to think that nothing else is needed. You may harbor a feeling that your peers, colleagues, and bosses behind big desks too will just figure out your capability and give you a pat on the back. Perhaps a promotion too. And when that doesn't happen you might blame the office politics, favoritism, unproductive work atmosphere, incompetent management, so on and so forth. But don't you think that the responsibility to impress with your talent, where and when needed, lies in your ability to communicate? You perhaps did not rise to the occasion and could not express yourself - clearly, cogently, and timely.

Friend, you can definitely do much better by realizing the importance of communication skills and equipping yourself with the best of it. Don't waste time - yours and of others. Become a life-long student of good and effective communication.

Why should I care about people's understanding!

You are fortunately connected to everybody driving the wheels of work and business. You have a full network of people, enabling you to work. Some are colleagues, some are peers, some are vendors, and some are clients, apart from the formal media and its infinite channels. So if you don't define your ambit of work, your ways, your solutions, and enable the next in line to make decisions; there's no progress. No progress for you or for the company. It is cyclical in nature - someone is enabling you, and you're enabling someone in turn. With focused and fulsome communication, the work will get done more efficiently and happily.

To understand and to be understood is the whole game plan for successful communication.

That's not my job!

Think again. Getting jobs done is your job. And what are your tools? It's words, emails, presentations, chats, interviews, memos, conferences, online meets, videos, audios, social media... and perhaps more are coming. But intrinsically, your knowledge, expertise, and information, have to find an expression; and you will have to choose one or more channels from the above.

What do I have to gain!

These are soft skills. Nice to be perceived as a good communicator, a good team player and all, but what do I have to gain? Whole lot. Success comes to those who work at it. With successful communication, you could build a good team for yourself. Clear communication will help you and others make purposive decisions. Time and efforts will be saved in rework, life will become productive and happy, and you can definitely see yourself advancing towards your career goals.

Short Stories for you: The Boss Has Changed

Once upon a time I had a boss, who was like this wicked witch. Always in a brisk snippy mood - sending me mails of work to be done on tight deadlines, not giving me any helpful resources, you get the idea. I had no idea what was in store for me at review time; and I saw no progression path in my career at the workplace.

And then one fine day it all changed. She started including me in inter-departmental meets, her mails had all the details of new clients and their timelines and how we should optimize resources, even asking me for my ideas and suggestions! And the best of all - she coached me through a mock review meeting before the final reviews and promotions sessions began, also guided me to make a document of my achievements at work. I saw that she had made a clear sparkling way for me to shine in my job. Wow my boss had changed!!

But don't we know what had changed? Her communication style! She was more inclusive, empathetic, detailed, sharing all information and knowledge, with timely and equitable communication. That day she won a productive and fully invested team member.

> "*"Life is an echo. What you send out, comes back. What you sow, you reap. What you give, you get. What you see in others, exists in you. Remember, life is an echo. It always gets back to you. So give goodness. Give clarity. Give direction. Give call for action. Emanate good communication"*"

You are what you communicate.

Empower yourself with Effective Communication.

I am willing to release all blocks to my creative expression and communication NOW!

CHAPTER FIVE

ARE YOU READY?

- Take the Communication Proficiency Indicator Test
- Create powerful Communication Goals
- Make them SMART: Specific, Measurable, Attainable, Realistic, Time-based

SMART Goal checklist

Are You Ready?

"Communication – the human connection – is the key to personal and career success."

Paul J. Meyer

Take the Communication Proficiency Indicator Test:

From the basic model of five elements of communication we talked about before - Sender, Message, Transmission and Noise, Receiver, Feedback we can expand to a more purposive model of seven elements:

Sender -----> Coding -----> Message ----> Channel Transmission ----> Noise Decoding ---->

Message ----> Receiver ----> Feedback

With everything remaining the same, the coding and decoding of the message and choice of channel will dictate the success of your message. Complete check of information being sent, the how's and why's in place, will help in complete understanding of your message and it will be decoded in the right context.

For each statement, tick the box in the column that best describes you:

1. I gather information about my topic before I launch into a debate, or I don't enter it:

- Not at all
- Rarely
- Sometimes

- Often
- Very Often

2. I listen with an open mind, even when I'm not in favor of the decision being taken, before I put my point of view:

- Not at all
- Rarely
- Sometimes
- Often
- Very Often

3. If I need to connect to an associate, I ask for the person's email id, in addition to their phone number:

- Not at all
- Rarely
- Sometimes
- Often
- Very Often

4. I share information with relevant people in my office group, timely and completely:

- Not at all
- Rarely
- Sometimes
- Often
- Very Often

5. I seek opportunity to discuss with my colleagues and seniors, when I'm in disagreement with their views:

- Not at all
- Rarely
- Sometimes
- Often
- Very Often

6. I envision anticipated discussions in times of disagreement, and frame cogent and intelligent responses beforehand:

- Not at all
- Rarely
- Sometimes
- Often
- Very Often

7. I watch out for people's body language when discussing contentious issues:

- Not at all
- Rarely
- Sometimes
- Often
- Very Often

8. I choose my words carefully when discussing change in operating rules of the organization, while talking to my team members:

- Not at all
- Rarely
- Sometimes
- Often

- Very Often

9. I make a personal note on the strengths of my point of view, before starting an important discussion:

   - Not at all
   - Rarely
   - Sometimes
   - Often
   - Very Often

10. I try to preempt possible causes of misunderstanding or confusion, and deal with it on forefront:

    - Not at all
    - Rarely
    - Sometimes
    - Often
    - Very Often

11. I proactively reach out to hurt audience - acknowledging their unhappiness and receiving their suggestions for possible ways of correction for future:

    - Not at all
    - Rarely
    - Sometimes
    - Often
    - Very Often

12. I am mindful in my choice of channel of communication as per the need, be it emails, interpersonal discussions, WhatsApp, printed documents/memos, or a formal

meeting:

- Not at all
- Rarely
- Sometimes
- Often
- Very Often

13. I seek feedback from peers and seniors or clients after presentations:

- Not at all
- Rarely
- Sometimes
- Often
- Very Often

14. When I have to take leave, I put it on email and wait for my boss' response:

- Not at all
- Rarely
- Sometimes
- Often
- Very Often

15. I check for an opportune time to present my case:

- Not at all
- Rarely
- Sometimes
- Often
- Very Often

Check out your Communication Proficiency Score and what it means:

Please assign yourself marks as defined below:

1 for Not at all, **2** for Rarely, **3** for Sometimes, **4** for Often, **5** for Very Often

Sum up your score and check your proficiency to being an Effective Communicator

15-35: There is a big scope to improve your communication skill. You are not sending or receiving the messages correctly. However, if you pursue reading and practicing good communication skills, you will be on your way to becoming an efficient communicator. This will translate into greater efficiency at work and happier relationships with your colleagues.

36-55: You are a capable communicator. However, you're having trouble at being received clearly. You need to go a step further and think about how your message is being received, and boost your communication capabilities. With some focused thought and practice of good communication principles you can overcome these obstacles. And reap rewards for being an able and efficient communicator - climb the ladder of success

56-75: You are a very efficient and effective communicator. You take due care whilst crafting, sending, and receiving a message. You are popular in your organization because of your good communication skills; also the clarity of your communication has helped boost productivity at your workplace.

Create Powerful Communication Goals:

We can create effective and powerful communication goals if we understand the elements of communication and their function. Communication does not end with just sending the message across. The successful transmission lies in listening to the response, which maybe coded verbally or non-verbally (like through body language). This will tell you whether your message landed correctly, and as you had intended.

Transfer your Communication Goals to paper

Now that's the commitment we are talking about. You can write at least five powerful communication goals like:

- I will make business strategy before I sit to work
- I will practice shooting emails with complete information at my work place
- I will cultivate the habit of listening for increased efficiency
- I will network with associates and clients
- I will learn new presentation techniques

Make them SMART: Specific, Measurable, Attainable, Realistic, Time-based

We are not done as yet. We have to make them SMART, to be able to track our progress and set new goals.

Specific: Make the goals as niche as possible. There is greater probability of achieving them. Also it provides sharper focus. Here's an example:

- I will make business strategy before I sit to work. I will research my topic and make notes for quick referring to industry growth patterns, so then I can make an impactful business strategy

Measurable: Make your goals measurable. You will be happy to see the advancement of your communication goal, on a set timeline. Or you can reset your goals, if you find yourself lagging. For example, it could be:

- I will practice shooting emails with complete information, at my work place. I will start my day with responding to all emails, so that everyone is equipped with information needed to carry out their tasks

Attainable: Attainment of goals leads to the rewards factory in our brain. You are motivated to set more challenging goals and advance further. But if you set unattainable or unachievable goals then reaching out for the goal may lead to frustration, and demotivate you. That would be a serious setback, and may set you in a loop of "I can't do anything or I am just not destined to be successful." So your goals should be well-crafted, an example:

- I will cultivate the habit of listening for increased efficiency. I will seek feedback from my friends and colleagues, also from my seniors post presentation

Realistic: The goals must be realistic. Having unrealistic expectation in a short time span is counter-productive and a waste of time. Check whether you have the resources: time, money, ability, willingness, people, and setting, before you chalk your goal, and set about achieving it. A realistic goal could read like:

- I will network with associates and clients. I will subscribe to business newspapers and journals, and have ready information resource to counsel my clients accordingly

Timely: Nothing gets done without putting the time parameter against it. To keep the goal effectual and relevant, you must include the time factor. An example of a timely goal:

- I will learn new presentation techniques on the two coming weekends of the month; so that I can integrate it in my business strategy, when the company is going to allocate new budgets for projects

And set positive affirmations, every single day. These are your secret weapons and can be one of your favorite tools too, for aligning your mindset with the direction of your goals and dreams.

I HAVE
WHAT IT
TAKES TO
REACH
MY GOALS

CHAPTER SIX

Organize Your Speech for Success

- Three parts of a Speech: Introduction, Body, Conclusion
- Create a Mind map
- Develop the Outline
- Why Outline
- Fill in the Outline
- Tips for Success
- Close it Right

Organize Your Speech for Success: Be a Master Storyteller

"The best speakers in the world are the best storytellers. They have a gift to not only tell a great story, but also share a lot of the details that many others wouldn't."

~ Larry Hagner

You know how you enjoy someone's company because they are master story tellers, and always tickle your imagination! Be that person. You will be surprised as to how many skills work in both the ambits: personal as well as professional.

Three parts of a Speech: Introduction, Body, Conclusion

Every speech and story has three critical components: Introduction, body and conclusion. For the understanding to flow right, you must use the right sequence too; in which instance you will be reiterating the purpose of your speech.

Introduce the subject to set the context. Present the body of your speech in an expressive way with examples, and perhaps anecdotes too. Learn to conclude your speech so that the message is reaffirmed in your audiences' mind. It is the mind which is the receptacle of all information and ideas.

Create a mind map:

This is the first step to success of your communication. Consider the mind map like a dump of all your thoughts leading to the speech and away from it. The purpose, the channel, the topic, the audience, the sensitivity, the probable obstructions, and the communication goal – all combine to make a mind map. You can either put it in a diagram or a written flowchart or even draw a freehand mind map with labels.

Why outline?

The outline helps you flesh out your point of view, response, speech, and presentation. It helps you nail any lacunae in the steps and shows you any gaps in communication. You will be much clearer and sorted if you have already developed an outline, also ready to lob responses that you believe in.

Develop the outline:

How do you ever get to your conclusion without developing an outline? Learn to develop an outline of your speech with a catchy introduction, engaging and insightful body, and a natural conclusion.

Fill in the outline:

Next, fill in the outline with an interesting hook to open your speech. A point of view supported with research, facts and figures, leading to a natural conclusion, helping the audience to travel along with you from start to finish. You will be surprised how a cohesive speech can persuade your audience to your point of view, even demolish many resistances along the way.

Close it Right!

Recap your biggest takeaway - reiteration in a logical way always works.

And remember to tie everything together; a summary would be useful. You could also share a success story - it reaffirms the points of your argument. Lastly and most importantly, do make a call-to-action - directly or indirectly. This is what you set about to: make changes in the course of action or propel someone to the next step.

See that you have been understood clearly, close communication gaps, and ask for feedback and queries.

Tips for Success: Nailing your What, Why, Who, How, When, is very important

- What is my communication goal? What is the purpose of my exercise?
- Why do I need it? Why is it important to me right now?
- Who is the target audience for my proposed communication?
- How will I convey my message? How will it come across?
- When should I schedule it? When is the right time?
- How did it go? Have I succeeded in my goal? What is to be done next?

These questions answer your entire communication query; and lead you closer to your advancement, growth in life, and at workplace.

> ***"To effectively communicate, we must realize that we are all different in the way we perceive the world and use this understanding as a guide to our communication with others."***

~ Anthony Robbins

“I am creative. My words flow easily and beautifully”

CHAPTER SEVEN

6 Keys to Effective Communication

- Set Your Objectives
- Understand Your Purpose
- Target your Audience
- What do they want
- What is a good time
- How to Achieve my Goal

Short Stories for You: Rise and shine, Aditya Biswas!

Six Keys to Effective Communication

"If all my possessions were taken from me with one exception, I would hope to keep my power of communication for by it I would regain all the rest"

- *Woody Allen*

Set Your Objectives: Effective communication begins with setting of clear objectives

Let's understand the flow through an example.

Understand the flow of your goal, purpose, audience, baselines, timeline, and index of success.

Objective:

- You want to have a team of your own for clearer and shorter command
- To avoid long and staggered chain of communication, and to avoid misunderstandings
- To have better results for your team and for yourself
- Deliver measurable success of your team
- Reap the benefits of enhanced productivity for yourself and your team members

Understand Your Purpose:

- To be more visible in the hierarchy line
- To have better prospects at promotion and career advancement
- To make a positive difference at workplace

Target Your Audience:

- Boss, Manager, Functional Head
- Team members

What do THEY want?

- Minimizing conflict at workplace
- Arranging harmonious job conditions for better work efficiencies
- Increasing productivity

What is a good time?

In this instance you have to seek audience with the decision maker- your Manager, and look out for the following situations:

- When reviewing work and timelines
- When reviewing new projects
- When reviewing increments and promotions

How to achieve my goal?

- Make the plan known to my team members, who are also my primary stakeholders
- Enlist their acceptance, by telling them the advantages of operating as a smaller niche group
- Team should be supportive and cheerleaders for the change
- Keep it confidential. You don't want cross winds to blow off the plan before it even sees the light of the day
- Seek appropriate opportunity, or seek time to sit with your manager to present your case
- Look for verbal and non-verbal feedback and response
- Note down if you have any reservations or need for additional information
- Send an email with bulleted points as to the advantages, the logistics of division, dispelling reservations, providing additional information, reaffirming faith in management, and their support for the plan ahead
- Lastly state your confidence in the plan and the support of the management. Close it on a note of positivity. Close it right!
- Follow it up. Don't forget to thank the decision-maker for reposing faith in your team
- Celebrate success with your team members
- Deliver as promised, it will entail a faster and positive response to your asks in the next round

Life is full of change - some you bring onto yourself, some happen, whichever! With the right communication you can always have better and happier results.

Short Stories for you: Rise and Shine, Aditya Biswas

And then we had a new hire in our team, Aditya Biswas. He was our Copy Editor for the marketing department. We were both dismayed and amused; as he couldn't speak proper English to save his life. There were glitches galore, the grammar was totally random, and his terrible misuse of words kept everybody in the spin. What did he mean now? "Mr. Rai is idle" and he was talking about the director! We figured after some time that Aditya meant that Mr. Rai is free right now and we could go for a talk. What an idling talk!

Unknown to us, Aditya was transforming himself from a raw recruit into a sharp professional. His previous place of work, an unorganized small business, did not give him the opportunity to nurture savvy communication practices. But now being at a structured corporate hub, where there was a place and opportunity for every talent, he took to some serious learning. He was reading Economic Times and business magazines, listening to BBC news, taking mental notes of any new term or usage, imbibing good practices of communication, writing blogs for practice, volunteering for any extra jobs around the department- sometimes even outside the department, practicing presentations, letting go of any fear of public speaking, setting communication goals every day... just grabbing all opportunities to improve his communication skills and overcoming all his anxieties of being seen in a poor light.

Aditya succeeded fabulously. We used to marvel at his confidence in offering to be the anchor speaker for meetings, sending us links to his blogs, proposing new media for communication, and how to go about it. And he proved us all wrong. Today he has books to his name, goes to felicitate honor students at IITs and management institutes, and is a known name as a motivational speaker.

Aditya knows the journey!!

> “***“If you just communicate, you can get by, but if you communicate skilfully, you can work miracles”***”

~ Jim Rohn

"I believe my communication skills are strong"

CHAPTER EIGHT

Say it Correctly!

- Use Right Grammar & Word Pronunciation
- Check Your Pronunciation

Short Stories for You: You inspire me, Aditi!

Say it Correctly!

"Your grammar is a reflection of your image. Good or bad, you have made an impression. And like all impressions, you are in total control."

- Jeffrey Gitomer

Use Right Grammar:

Right ideas work with the right grammar. Poor grammar and incorrect spellings reflect a poor version of you. It says that you did not take the help of an app, a peer, or a learner's course to improve your media of expression; it erodes your credibility. It also adds to the scope of confusion and general irritation. Your ideas may evoke undesirable reactions like laughter or sarcasm, and the intent and worth of the idea is lost.

Please take care to improve your language of communication. Check and proofread in case of written communication before hitting the SEND button. At least, you know that your idea has reached the sender in clear language; and that the decision-maker appreciates crisp correct messages. It is a bullet-proof way of saving time and effort, to share information and showcase your ideas.

- Enroll in a learner's course if necessary
- Check for correct grammar via apps and other resources

- Enlist help to read or listen to your messages and incorporate change, until you gain confidence in tackling it on your own

Check Your Pronunciation:

Don't lose the message with wrong pronunciation. You may lose the audience too with poorly pronounced words. The receiver may get irritated with poor pronunciations, especially of critical words, and time and productivity both will be lost.

To learn correct pronunciation and keep on the path of learning you should:

- Check online resources for the correct pronunciation

- Listen to English News
- Hear from your peers
- Record your speech and listen to it- for flow of words, grammar, and pronunciation
- Look for glitches, or which words sound odd to you
- Check and rectify, wherever needed
- Substitute words which make you habitually stumble over them
- Foreign proper nouns and words should be rehearsed for correct and smooth flow
- Seek feedback from others
- Goalpost is complete or near complete fluency in the chosen language for communication

"Communication is your ticket to success, if you pay attention and learn to do it effectively."
Theo Gold

Short Stories for You: You inspire me, Aditi!

An ode to the best colleague I have had - Aditi Prasad. She was sharp at her work, never missing a deadline, and always on top of every project and event at the organization. But what made her a perfect colleague to me? She would simplify complex for me, things that would escape my understanding, she would unravel for me; and then she had these wonderful traits which I benefitted from - she could relate to me and my predicaments at work, she would listen to me, she had confidence, she was specific and clear in her communication, she was focused on outcomes, she could speak up and was a natural leader when it came to difficult situations... She had practiced on tools of communication and improved on it daily.

Yes, Aditi was the perfect communicator. And worked at it diligently.

I have a rich vocabulary and add to it daily

CHAPTER NINE

Understand Body Language: Way to Non-verbal Communication

- Actions speak louder than Words
- Pay Attention to Your Appearance, Gestures & Expressions
- 7 Body Language Tips for Success

Understand Body Language: Way to Non-verbal Communication

Albert Mehrabian, a pioneer researcher of body language in the 1950's, found that the total impact of a message is about ***7 percent*** *verbal (words only) and* ***38 percent*** *vocal (including tone of voice, inflection, and other sounds) and* ***55 percent*** *non-verbal. It's how you looked when you said it, not what you actually said.*

"I speak two languages: Body and English. "

~ Mae West

Theorists say that over 50% of your communication is non-verbal. Now that's a lot! Don't underestimate the power of non-verbal communication; it is what propels your ideas to the next step. Body language includes - your posture, gestures, facial expressions, eye contact, which add meaning to your words. When in sync, verbal and non-verbal communication support each other and help deliver message successfully.

Actions Speak Louder than Words:

You are in the client's cabin asking for more resources for an ongoing project. Sitting straight in your chair, with your hands clasped lightly in front of you, and a smile reflected in your eyes; you have already conveyed to the client that they are dealing with a positive and confident person. This affirmative body language of yours boosts the message and has a high chance of getting a "Yes" for an answer. But had you clenched your fists, raised your eyebrows, shaken your head in negation, then the body language would have conveyed something else altogether: aggressive state of mind, perhaps unstable and emotional; and the client would naturally think that a critical decision cannot be taken in this state of incoherence. You would have lost the client's trust. The purpose of the meeting would be defeated. So if you want the meeting to go your way, make the body language express accordingly.

You have to set your body language right, so that it sends a positive and affirmative message to the person sitting across. And the point is near to being accepted. There has to be a match between the content of your message to the mood being conveyed by your body language.

Your body is an instrument of your speech.

Pay Attention to Your Appearance, Gestures & Expressions:

What's with formals for conferences? And casuals for Friday dressing? Your appearance makes you. It also sets the mood for the meeting. These are critical and telling factors; they tell more about you than you would have reckoned with - that you have taken care to dress accordingly, you are a neat and organized person, you look to details, and hopefully have aesthetics which you can translate at the workplace. Who can quibble with aesthetics, in business or even in passion? Most things give a jolt of happiness when packaged aesthetically. Poor or untidy appearance, of course, reflects conversely on your personality and way of doing things. Help the person make their decision in your favor with an apt appearance.

Gesturing is movement with any part of your body, especially your hands - to convey or reinforce a message. Gesture definitely adds to your message, if controlled and purposive.

This small list gives an idea of which gestures are avoidable:

- Avoid distracting movements like: Rocking, Swaying, or Pacing
- Gripping or leaning on the table
- Tapping the fingers or biting the lips

The Facial Expressions are visual data on attitudes, feelings, and emotions. How many times do we look at ourselves and rehearse before an important interview? The mirror is our true counsellor. Or even video recording. It tells us in an infallible tone that we need to smile, hold that gaze, nod in agreement, and sit with shoulders squared. Combined with positive pleasant gestures and facial expressions, you would have equipped your arsenal of tools for effective communication.

7 Body Language Tips for Success:

1. Body Posture: Position your body confidently
2. Your Body Movement: Reassuring and calm
3. Gestures: Support your words, dramatize your ideas, make it natural & spontaneous
4. Facial Expressions: Pleasant, no frowning or irritating mannerisms
5. Eye Contact: Make your presentations direct & personal; establish a bond with eye contact
6. Appearance: Neat and apt for the occasion, personal style adds up to it
7. Build Self-Confidence through preparation

Your purpose is to enhance your natural, spontaneous, and conversational style. But you have to prepare for it every time. Use Communication as a Learning Laboratory.

The most important thing in communication is to hear what isn't being said.
- Peter F. Drucker

"I ensure that my body language reflects the words I am speaking"

CHAPTER TEN

How to Make a Good First Impression

- Create a Visual Presentation
- Dress to Impress
- Display a Positive Outlook
- Listen Attentively
- Exceed Expectations
- Be that Successful Communicator

Short Stories for You: Dress it up like Nymph Kaul!

How to Make a First Good Impression

"Every time you have to speak, you are auditioning for Leadership "

~ James Humes

Why are we so anxiety ridden on our first meeting? First date? First round of interview? When we knock on the door of the client we have been pursuing through calls for three months?

It's the anxiety of First Impression. If you nail it on the first go, then your work becomes so much easier.

You have made detailed presentations, you have made business strategies, and outcome models. You have mailed all of the above and answered every query. You have also mailed-in your or your company's profile. Your written and verbal communication is on point. And still we wait for the climax - for the meeting in person or on camera. And that decides it all. No wonder it is said that the First Impression is your Last Impression.

Create a Visual Presentation:

First Impression is a visual presentation of you, of the brand YOU. Folks make a judgement based on what they are seeing. In addition to the product, service, or the idea which they have liked, they are also happy or in tune with the presenter.

The onus is on you to help your target audience take the next step.

Dress to Impress:

Your sense of dressing takes you a long way in getting the recognition and respect you deserve. It also reflects a sense of style. And builds the brand - YOU. Dressing doesn't mean going overboard but suiting to the occasion and amping up your style. There are various studies that indicate that the opening you are looking for is facilitated by your power dressing; it also helps in subsequent promotions and perks. Good dressing and grooming is a reflection, of your image and the confidence you exude.

As we said, you are what you communicate.

Shoddy or poor dressing leads to cognitive dissonance - where the person looking to invest in you is impressed with the qualifications and experience you bring to the table, but is not able to comprehend the reason for your slovenly appearance. Remove this mismatch and let your talent find its true worth by impactful dressing.

Display a Positive Outlook:

Managing situations and challenges with an optimistic outlook is an attitude we all look out for. Positive attitude and outlook convey confidence and happiness quotient and boosts your image with the receiver. It shows that you are not self-limiting in your beliefs, you have an open personality, you are a problem solver, and that you are an asset in tough situations as you manage life with positivity.

You are empowering, upbeat, and enthusiastic - all traits which communicate right with the decision maker.

Of all the things you wear, the most important is your expression.

Listen Attentively:

> ***"*"We have two ears and one tongue so that we would listen more and talk less."* ”**

~ Diogenes

How often have we heard of that? Why do we forget that communication is a two-way process? The job is not complete by just sending a deftly crafted message; it needs to resonate with the target audience, and that happens when they receive it and respond to it. If they respond in the way that you intended, then it is good communication. The loop of communication is then complete, and now it's your turn to listen to it and respond appropriately. Receive, reflect, and respond. That's the *mantra* of ever going communication.

In this high-tech, high-speed, high-stress world, listening is increasingly the better part of communication. Lot of times the opportunity and message gets lost because we are not listening. So intent are we to have our say, that we have missed all verbal and non-verbal cues.

And the communication ends up all garbled, and is a waste of time.

To cultivate being a Good Listener, you should strive to be:

- Empathetic

- Focused
- Open-minded
- Relaxed
- Helpful, but not intrusive
- Observant and adaptive

Remember, it is not a contest of who gets in the last word. You are trying to cultivate bonds; to impress upon the other that you have wide understanding but only to help the person in the current situation. *Give that person regular feedback that you are listening!*

Exceed Expectations:

Yes, of course: Be the best version of yourself, and more. Think intuitively as to what is required of you in the current situation - a listener, a problem-solver, a team player, a leader, a decision-maker; and communicate to remove all doubts, and impress with your ability and attitude. Don't think that opportunities will come your way and you just have to be yourself. You have to be better than yourself, and your communication skills need to shine.

Nothing succeeds like success, as they say.

Be that Successful Communicator:

You know the skills, and now it is karma time. Be alive and alert to all the communication tools in your arsenal. If you don't practice, those tools will rust. You may be in a tough situation currently, needing to present yourself to the new top boss; think of it as a case study with a little detachment. Sometimes it makes for a good lesson as you look at the situation in third person; studying which factors helped the situation and which communication tool could have been better used and how for a successful outcome of the situation.

Be patient, be an active listener, be that pro-active communicator, and check for gains.

Short Stories for You: Dress it up like Nymph Kaul!

"Style is a way to say who you are without having to speak."

~Rachel Zoe

You remember the story of the frog and princess where the princess kissed the ugly frog and he transformed into a charming Prince??

Well that happens in real life too! I have seen it happen in front of my eyes.

The department was full of petty office politics, rife with rumors and little productivity, professionalism was unheard of and projects were making very little headway.

Then in strode a very striking lady with elegance to match her professional stature. Nymph Kaul, Marketing Director, became an icon of both style and substance. Draped in sharp ethnic sarees, she gave the office the dignity it deserved. The accessories she wore, the lemon teas she sipped, the polished way of speaking... and most importantly, the professionalism she brought in transformed the ugly frog into a charming prince, at a go. The department sparkled under her charge.

The Style Diva had wrought a change. Never underestimate the synergy of style and substance at work.

"You never get a second chance at making a first impression"

"I easily command my audience's attention"

CHAPTER ELEVEN

Energize Your Talk with Vocal Variety

- Remember the 4 Ps of good communication: Pace, Pitch, Pause, Passion
- How well do you Articulate
- Increase Your Vocal Variety

Short Stories for You: Mr. Machado strikes all the right notes!

Energize Your Talk with Vocal Variety

"Words mean more than what is set down on paper. It takes the human voice to infuse them with deeper meaning."

~ Maya Angelou

Have you ever tried to escape a monotonous drone? Doctors say that most of the Pharmaceutical Salesmen are so poorly trained in communications that in those 10 minutes granted to them, they set upon a monologue of the description and benefits of the drug, without checking even once whether they have been understood. Or is the doctor even interested in it. With a flat tone, and absolutely no enthusiasm, the representative sets upon the task of talking about the company's product. This is indeed unproductive communication. It would have benefitted them, and given a boost to their presentation, if it was infused with vocal variety. The listener engagement is important.

Any sentence with variation in the inflection of the voice will convey a different meaning. Consider this "Don't go to the party dressed like this" sounds like a flat sentence with a flat meaning. But as per your vocal emphasis, the implied meaning of the sentence will change.

Check it out:

"**Don't** go to the party dressed like this" (Sounds authoritative: You can't go)

"Don't **go** to the party dressed like this" (Sounds contemplative: Perhaps you shouldn't be)

"Don't go to the **party** dressed like this" (Sounds incredulous: Can't be for the party surely!)

"Don't go to the party **dressed** like this" (Sounds judgmental: Dressing is important)

"Don't go to the party dressed like **this**" (Downright thumbing down: You have an atrocious sense of dressing)

So just with tonal variation and intonation, the meaning conveyed is very different. And so will be the response. Understandably, you have to tailor your tone to get the desired response and action. Listen to your voice.

Remember the 4 Ps of Vocal Variety for good communication: Pace, Pitch, Pause, Passion:

How do you catch your client's attention? The presentation is much the same. But what makes a difference is you and the energy you present it with. Remember to integrate the 4Ps of vocal variety here:

- Pace: Are you fast or slow; the speed of your talk
- Pitch: Are you loud or soft; the decibel of your talk
- Pause: Are you talking incessantly; the suitable breaks in your talk
- Passion: Are you enthusiastic or listless: the energy in your talk

Remember to use the 4Ps for effect and impact. Vary the pace, as per the content of your speech, to enhance the feel of your speech. Emphasize important terms and words with deeper and slower tonality, to let them sink in the audience's mind, and for better recall. You can be relatively faster during narration.

Similarly, the pitch must also be adjusted to have the audience clued in to your talks. Use the story telling technique of varying between constant, loud, and soft, for engaging the audience.

Pauses are critical as you give nano-breaks in your talk for impact; also to give time to audience to reflect and digest it.

Now what would you do without passion? You have a job of transmitting that passion and enthusiasm for your ideas to the audience. And for this, it is important that everything comes together - the content of your speech, how you say it, the apt skills of your verbal and non-verbal communication, and your body language.

Increase Your Vocal Variety:

Rehearse, practice, and audition yourself with either friends or peers, or coaches, or even recording devices; this is the only way to check your progress in using an increased vocal variety. The final result should be a nuanced delivery of your speech - with emphasis at the right places, strategic pauses for impact, additional engagement of the audience with varying decibel of your talk sometimes; and boosting the whole experience with visible enthusiasm.

How well do you Articulate:

With social media being the most frequent channel of communication nowadays, people have lost practice of crafting a well expressed response. Articulation is the skill of putting your thoughts across in a concise and clear manner. It requires alertness to absorb the given information and deep analytical skills to process and respond without much delay.

Some people fumble when asked to articulate their response; it could be written or verbal. And some people have the gift of quick understanding; they give value added response which is also a call to action.

Some phrases which can help get attention quickly and purposively are:

- Need your advice
- Design proposals for your consideration
- Need a quick review
- Do you want to go ahead on this?
- Help! There is a problem
- What course of action do you suggest?

Using such phrases as your theme lines or subject lines grabs the audience attention, and is a direct call for action. Use them with caution, and only in relevant scenarios.

This is the right time to add the role of active listening too. It helps to adapt your response to the message received, in the right context.

If there is a communication club or a public speaking forum in your city, consider joining it. Nowadays there are proficient online forums too. These prove to be a good arena for experiential learning and practicing public speaking skills. Complete with feedback. Even if pursued for short periods, there would be a measurable difference in your speaking skills.

Short Stories for You: Mr. Machado strikes all the right notes!

Mr. Machado, my first boss at Pidilite, was a perfect match for striking all the right notes. One welcomed the opportunity to be called to his cabin even when one knew that the session would entail being pulled up for not adhering to a deadline. He ensured that even in a reprimand he bolstered your self-esteem. Have you ever known such a person? He could deliver his message without raising his voice - smoothly and with full conviction. The person always left his cabin thinking, *Yes, Mr. Machado has a point*. He always did, such was his finesse with communication.

"I am smart. I am powerful. My voice can make a difference"

CHAPTER TWELVE

Boost Your Speech with Visual Aids

- Get Comfortable with Visual Aids
- Powerful Tools for Complex Ideas

Boost Your Speech with Visual Aids

"Well-designed visuals do more than provide information; they bring order to the conversation."

~ Dale Ludwig and Greg Owen-Boger

Visual Aids are a big category of formal and informal props, devices, and drawings. They support your spoken and written words by adding meaning and information to your message. Think of a manual of a coffee making machine you have just bought. You need to know where to put the milk and where to add the coffee powder; the written instructions may or may not be there, but the visual steps with labels are all that you need to know. Even if written in Chinese.

Visual Aids include:

- PowerPoint Presentation or something similar
- Overhead projector slides/transparencies
- Mind maps
- Manuals with drawings
- White or black board
- Brochures
- Flow charts
- Financial charts
- Video clips
- Artefacts or props
- Hand drawn illustrations

"The brain processes visual information 60,000 times faster than text."

The visual aids are useful to transmit your information in an interesting and impactful way. Statistics say that visual retention goes much farther than hearing or reading, and helps the brain save the meaning of the message.

Powerful Tools for Complex Ideas:

Visual Aids should be an important weapon in your arsenal of communication, as it targets effective communication in many ways:

- **Helps quick and complete information processing:** Some things are best supported with Visual Aids like graphs of growth - where the line and parameters tell the story at a go. And then it is easier to follow the nitty-gritties of the company's growth with facts and figures, accompanying the graph
- **Helps in retaining and recalling information**: Let's think of an ACRONYM which is also mental and visual aid, for remembering a complex set of useful information. Think of SMART and the cues will come automatically – Specific, Measurable, Attainable, Realistic, Time-based
- **Overcomes barriers of Language**: That is why most Made in China appliances come with NO written text; just step by step pictures of components and their assembly for operation. Nobody needs to learn Chinese and China doesn't need to know your language. *Eureka!*
- **Helps in saving time for absorbing information:** Think of the unending hours and talks required to present a new national highway; being built at a great cost,

without showing the strategic importance by mapping it visually. All arts of war and peace need visual representation for greater impact and understanding

- **Avoids brain fatigue by using the Multichannel approach:** The brain has different areas for processing different kinds of information: the written, the oral, and the visual. By using the multichannel approach, you are increasing the probability of critical information reaching the target audience; the reader or listener's brain doesn't suffer unnecessary fatigue by processing feed through only one type of channel
- **Avoids information overload:** Using a variety of communication channels, no particular channel will get blocked; and it will facilitate easy flow of message
- **Breaks down complex and layered information into digestible bytes:** Let's take the example of ***Ikigai***: the Japanese concept of channeling your inner calling and zest for life; the elements which matter in your life like passion, vocation, mission, profession, what you can contribute to the world, and what the world needs converge into an essence of your life called Ikigai. Ikigai shows direction or purpose in your life, showing you a path towards fulfillment. Isn't the written word here proving to be burdensome, complicated, and quite unexciting? Now let's look at the visual representation, and for sure Ikigai will make you feel inspired and alive.

> *"Tell me and I will forget. Show me and I may remember, involve me and I learn."*

~Benjamin Franklin

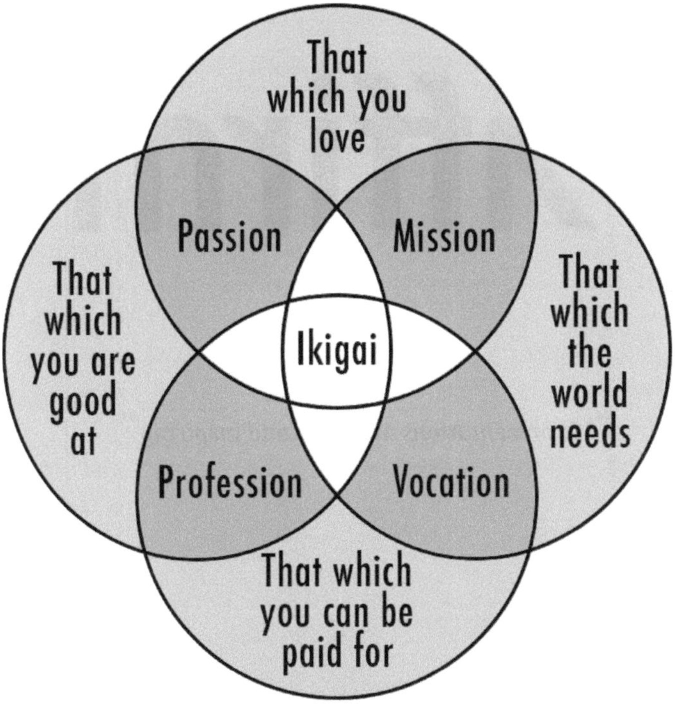

That which you love

Passion

Mission

That which you are good at

Ikigai

That which the world needs

Profession

Vocation

That which you can be paid for

IKIGAI: So now understand the true meaning of Ikigai.
Hope you find yours!

Affirm

"My presentations are clear and inspiring"

CHAPTER THIRTEEN

Research Your Topic

- Collect information from wide variety of sources
- Collect, Collate & carefully support your Topic

Research Your Topic

"The thing that makes me more attractive is I speak to the point and with facts and figures!"

~Thebrandboy.com

Your information is as good as your research. It is the foundation of the study you are preparing; this study can be used to persuade people to your suggestions, in written or spoken word. Research gives credibility and authority to your voice; of course, your sources have to be authentic and recognized in the field of study.

Research is categorized at three subsequent stages:

Primary Research: Is objective information coming from the first source; facts, figures and tabulated findings of a study - like in government journals, medical studies, or autobiographies, memoirs, etc. This is without much analytical commentary and has not been modified by any other writer or researcher

Secondary Research: Is subjective information - which means interpretations, analysis, views and opinions based on primary research. So this research is once removed from the original study

Tertiary Research: Is repackaged information; there's nothing original about it. Mostly no credit to the author is given either. These include compilation, indexing, organizing, or abstracting data.

Collect information from wide variety of sources:

Your presentation of ideas, thoughts, projects, and arguments, should be as solid as the research behind it. You must validate your POV (Point of View) with research from credible and verifiable sources; and then weave the facts, figures, and findings into your speech. It propels the reader or the listener in the direction of your thought and POV.

Remember to use a wide variety of sources to collect information and not depend on a single source. Whenever you state your POV, support it with well-researched statistics and findings; do not assume that the target audience will be able to link it on their own.

Many different types of sources exist for research that may be relevant to your speech topic. Those include journals, periodicals, newspapers, interviews, autobiographies, books, reference tools, online databases, and websites. It is important that you know how to evaluate the credibility of each type of source material.

Collect, Collate & carefully support your Topic:

The important research material collected must be collated to help deliver the desirable result and POV. Collating or organizing your data in an effective and efficient manner is necessary for it to become a tool for supporting your POV; also giving it lends clarity to the audience. A good spoken or written speech, where you want to either change perception or is a call for action, is always backed by research.

Research is an important element amongst the various support materials to be used in your speech. They include examples, explanations, statistics, analogies, testimony, and visual aids.

"All I'm armed with is research." -Mike Wallace

“I turn pending arguments into enriching discussions”

CHAPTER FOURTEEN

Assess & Evaluate Your Speech: Track Your Progress

- Importance of Feedback
- Was the topic well-researched?
- How well did you support your main points?
- How clear was your purpose?
- Was the speech effectively organized?
- Did you take advantage of body language and vocal variety?

Assess & Evaluate Your Speech:

Track Your Progress

"You can have brilliant ideas but if you can't get them across, your ideas won't get you anywhere."

~ ***Lee Iococca***

Have you seen the intricate workings of your smartphone camera equipped with an automatic flash? When you switch the phone to camera mode, the device continuously takes feedback from its surroundings to adjust the light settings and use the flash, if required. The built-in auto-sensors gather information and analyze data so that the pictures taken are sharp and vivid. The smartphone camera screen also lets you know the focus area by highlighting it in a yellow square. This interactive feedback between the user and the device is the reason that, rest assured, you will get a memorable picture. The more advanced the camera, the more fluid and fast the feedback integration works; it is also more 'sensory' feature-rich to give you enhanced 3D photos of high resolution. This all happens because of accurate and focused feedback. The continuous tracking of ambient factors is critical to the camera, for it to be reliable and deliver exceptional pictures.

The importance of feedback is woven into the yarn of communication. As we had earlier stated that communication is a two-way process: sending a well-crafted message, and being received at the other end with the same encoded meaning, with zero or minimum deviation. The loop continues with response from the receiver, which is feedback for you, and a signal for you to adjust the next message accordingly. The feedback can be positive or negative or status quo; and you can track your progress with this loop.

Importance of Feedback:

We have seen that feedback is critical for any progress to be made on the communication platform - be it written or spoken; or even social media, where the currency is the number of likes and followers. Let us investigate how feedback helps in the realm of communication:

Feedback is a Problem Solver: It helps build a consensus as conflicts are minimized; with every loop of sending and receiving information, and building in feedback at every successive stage, the common ground is easier to approach. Without feedback and adapting your message accordingly, the situation has a potential to get out of control

Feedback is Democratic: It engages the other group or person, and is participative. It shows the other person that their opinion is valuable too, and builds conducive environment to resolve the problem

Feedback helps Goalsetting: When the vison is setting an achievable goal, then feedback is important to check its viability, timeliness, and clarity

Feedback facilitates Coordination: Any plan of action requires the buy-in of other agencies; with feedback a well-coordinated and synchronized plan can be chalked out

Feedback is Constructive: It is important to both give and receive feedback for constructive purposes, to take a plan ahead, or improve in a given area. Since communication is a two-way process, no progress can be made without positive feedback

Feedback indicates area of Improvement: When received with an open mind, feedback helps in strengthening the weak points of a plan or POV. The sender gathers the receiver's opinions and views, and integrates those points to take the plan a step ahead.

In this context I would like to recommend the Oreo cookie approach for giving feedback: begin with giving credit for points well stated, sandwich it with room for improvement, and end it with encouragement and motivation. The two chocolate wafers of praise and boosting are held together with the light creamy filling of room for improvement.

Let us extrapolate some critical parameters to track the progress of your communication skills.

Was the topic well researched?

In other words - did you support your work, written or spoken, with formal and informal research sources? Did you talk to enough people in the field and collated your information to get to the deduction? If the answer is yes to both the questions above, then that is a definite uptick for progress in communication.

How well did you support your main points?

Did your plan of action, or project presentation, or POV, have ample support from your content? Did it all sound coherent and productive? And if you answer to the above two questions is positive, then you can add another uptick to your communication skills.

How clear was your purpose?

Did you seek feedback from the receiver, without thinking that it may be negative or positive or just some points added, or a caution note? Did you check whether your message was received with clear points? We are in the right direction if you said 'Yes' to the above two. This is definitely called Progress.

Was the speech effectively organized?

Did your speech have a clear structure of a beginning, middle, and an ending? Was the flow smooth and understandable to your audience? Again if yes, to both of the above, then you are much closer to being an effective communicator.

Did you take advantage of body language and vocal variety?

Were your actions, gestures, and facial expressions in sync with your message? Were you able to infuse your speech with vocal variety of pitch, pace, pause, and passion? A 'Yes' to these makes you an efficient and effective communicator.

These demonstrate that you are alert to the tools of communication and are using them mindfully and purposively.

Now you can recalibrate your communication skills and track your progress. Of course, one is assuming that you have been an active practitioner of the skills learnt here. *Karma* and *Dharma* go hand-in-hand (where *Karma* is your action ground and *Dharma* is your faith in principles, as per Hindu philosophy). The famous Bhagwad Gita is an entire communication between the mentor Krishna and the warrior prince Arjuna about the ethos of living.

According to Gita, effective communication is that which contains the truth, which is beneficial to the listener, pleasant to hear, and which is made only after self-study.

I only take part in positive conversations

CHAPTER FIFTEEN

MASTERING THE ART OF PERSUASION: TOP EIGHT MUST-DO'S

Written by Rajita Majumdar

About Rajita Majumdar:

Rajita is an international communications specialist, writer, world traveler and a curator of holistic living. Rajita has been spearheading communications strategies and product development for 20 years to advance missions of international nonprofits, government programs, and private-sector enterprises within the U.S. and globally. Her work has spanned across over 40 countries, largely focused on promoting and enabling sustainable development. In her personal time, Rajita is channelizing her global insights to bring nuggets of India's heritage on appealing, authentic platforms. She is based in the Washington DC area in the U.S.

Mastering the Art of Persuasion: Top Eight Must-Do's

> "*If you would persuade, you must appeal to interest rather than intellect.*"

~Benjamin Franklin

Do you realize we are "selling" our ideas all the time to make things happen the way we want to? Whether it's convincing your friend to go out for Japanese food rather than Chinese or telling your colleague at work to support your decision at office. Advertisements are another everyday example of persuasion – persuading you to buy a product or try out a service.

Learning the art of persuasion can unlock a world of opportunities and relationships for you and put you on a ladder of success. But how do you mater the art of persuasion?

Take a dive into your recent past and think of examples where you were persuaded to take an action and try to answer these questions:

Q. Why did you agree to try something new or pick a certain new product from the shelf or purchase it in the grocery store?

Q. What part of the communication stuck with you the most?

Q. Why did that message appeal to you?

Q. If you didn't buy into someone's suggestion, what lacked in the message or manner to convince you?

A self-analysis will reveal to you that successful persuasion always harnesses the power of both emotional and intellectual appeal to connect to its audiences. However, their relative use in persuasive communication varies depending on the nature of the ask, the outcomes from the decision, and the people involved in the negotiation.

Following are eight ways to enhance your persuasive communication skills:

1. **Be convinced of your initiative or topic before you approach others.** You can only persuade others if you truly believe in it yourself. Having a passion for the subject will make you work harder to build your case.
2. **Know your audiences and their needs.** To convince your listeners or readers, you must know whom you are talking to first – what interests them and what are their pain points. For example, if you want to propose a new activity that will benefit your company but the company is on tight budget, make sure you address cost concerns.
3. **Hook your audience's attention from the get-go.** The first step in persuasion is making them believe that what you are saying is worth listening to. Use a shocking statistic or a story with a human touch that links to your topic to grab attention.
4. **Appeal to the intellect** – do thorough research to build your case from both sides. Using evidence and examples of real-life experience builds your case and makes it more convincing. Always use credible sources of information if researching on the internet. Presenting your case from both sides—what will be the outcomes if audiences agree and what if they don't—positions you solidly to win your point. People listen to those who

demonstrate critical thinking and are able to address the pros and cons. For example, if you are selling health insurance, along with details of benefits, show the potential average out-of-pocket expenses for an average person if the customer doesn't buy the insurance.

5. **Appeal to emotions** – factor in human interest and be empathetic in your presentation. Using angles or examples that your readers or listeners can relate to makes your case stick and encourages more positive response. Using the same example of selling health insurance, weave in an unfortunate scenario of a family member diagnosis and how having health insurance will save unplanned costs and ensure peace of mind for the family.
6. **Recap with clear call to action at the end**. Reiterating your message and the rationale at the end is a strategic way to remind the audience of needed action or decision. Keep it creative, paraphrase, or end with a small anecdote or metaphor or quote to reinforce your point and not sound redundant. You could use a graphic or a visual aid to drive home the call to action.
7. **Use tone and body language to engage audiences**. Modulate your voice when delivering your speech or presentation and make direct eye contact with your audiences to keep their attention. If presenting in front of a large audience, make sure to move around a bit to cover the full room and to keep the audience interested. Use hand movements to emphasize or animate your points.
8. **Practice, practice, practice**. To appear confident and ensure sound delivery of your speech, practice it at least 2-3 times. You could practice in front of a mirror or with a colleague. Prepare a script or, at a minimum, jot

down opening statement, key points, and the ending. You don't want to appear faltering or doubtful when trying to persuade your audience.

As an extra, **consider humor in your speech!** That is if it's appropriate for the audience and the context. Humor relaxes up your audience and makes them more receptive to your messages.

Humor 'oils' the way,
reduces friction,
reduces barriers,
provides an energy in the room.

But remember, humor can be good or bad. Always keep it in good taste and sensitive to your audience.

Persuasion is an art, not a science.

I can influence people with my communication abilities!

CHAPTER SIXTEEN

Countdown to Becoming a Successful Communicator!

- The Six Principles of Persuasion: The Foundation
- The Five Steps of Persuasion: From Attention to Adoption
- The Four Channels of Persuasion: Formal and Informal
- The Three Types of Persuasion: Booster Dose
- The Two Strategies of Persuasion: Maslow's Hierarchy of Needs and Motivations
- Hit the Bullseye! Achieve your Goal

Countdown to becoming a Successful Communicator!

"The art of communication is the language of leadership."

~ James Humes

The Six Principles of Persuasion: The Foundation

Dr. Robert Cialdini, the social scientist of immense fame and called - The Godfather of Influence, has laid down six fundamental principles of persuasion, and these are easy and logical to follow:

1. Reciprocity
2. Commitment & Consistency
3. Social Proof
4. Liking
5. Authority
6. Scarcity

Reciprocity: If you offer a product or service, or a kind deed to a person, the goodwill generated and the idea of being indebted will work in your favor. People, in general, reciprocate kindness with kindness, generosity with generosity; especially if it is coming with a personal message and an exclusive offer.

Reciprocity is the most basic and intuitively used tool for persuasion. You eat at a restaurant and the restaurant gives you coupons for good reviews on Social Media.

You can make this principle of Reciprocity work for YOU by:

- Making an exclusive offer
- Being the first to offer
- Personalize the offer

Commitment and Consistency: If you have committed to the Organic movement and its subsequent call for action, then your list of purchases will show organic products. The marketers find this to be the easiest way of converting an existing group, under their choice of product or service category, to their particular offer. It is the least resistance method.

Social Proof: The root of this lies in the 'belonging' category. If your friends, or peers, or party members (can be political affiliation too) wear a certain dress code, or use certain product categories then you also want to follow suit. It's also called Herd Mentality in common terms. Like, for example, if CFOs (Chief Financial Officers) wear black suits to important meetings, there is a high chance of a new entrant to finance profession also wearing a black suit, in conformity. It is like a badge which says, this is where I belong!

Liking: As basic as that. You tend to get converted or persuaded by people or organizations you like. You are registered (in psychological terms) with them and receive information from them with an open mind. Vice versa when you appeal to your friends or people who are bonded to you, your message will have a path of least resistance.

Authority: If you have earned authority in your subject, or field of knowledge and operation, then your message carries undeniable weight. And that puts you on a pedestal of being an influencer. Your credibility score rises, in apparent cases, like being an eye doctor and talking about dangers of glaucoma or counselling someone on timeliness of a cataract operation ... Or let's say the head of marketing at Google, advising a startup on their social media strategy.

Scarcity: 'Limited supply' or 'for limited time only', or 'for limited viewership', or 'for limited people' – this sort of appeal of getting an exclusive deal, not available on a general scale, has immense scope for persuasion and conversion. This category includes early bird discounts, club memberships, elite subscriptions, and similar offers.

These six principles cover almost every type of persuasion, and sometimes are overlapping in nature. The impact multiplies accordingly. Think about British Airways offering a free two-day tour package in London, as bonus, with every purchase of full fare business class ticket booked on international route during the Christmas week. Authority, Scarcity, Reciprocity, perhaps Liking, is all in-built in that offer to persuade you to use their airline.

The Five Steps of Persuasion: From Attention to Adoption

1. Aim for the Audience Goal; state the purpose of your persuasion
2. Analyze the listeners needs and motivations; use their profile
3. Align your message to the receiver's motivation; apply the matrix of appeals

4. Arrange your message; create the impact with visualization, tonality, content, credibility, timing
5. Actualize it; deliver your message and evaluate it's success

If your belief, ideas or products/services have been adopted, you have been a successful persuader!

The communication exercise may need to go through another loop, if you see gap in the desired persuasion objective. Check if the message needs reiteration, follow-up or change of communication strategy.

The Four Channels of Persuasion: Formal and Informal

Your choice of channel, from amongst the available channels of communication, will depend on your persuasion goal. Each channel has a different fit - as per situation, the target audience, and the current need. Mass Media is an array of channels used to communicate to the masses, in a short time. These mass media channels, which multiply your message exponentially, comprise of Radio, Films, TV, Newspaper, Magazines, Journals, Flyers, Outdoor billboards, Signage on trains and like, and includes Digital Media too like Websites, Email, Social Media sites. So if you are going to persuade the country on hygiene and cleanliness issues like in the *Swachh Bharat* campaign, then use of Mass Media is the best. Or if you have a product to sell - like a Life Insurance Policy - then again Mass Media is of immense use in disseminating information to a large audience across the board.

However, in your day-to-day business of persuading your target audience, you may not require mass media as your channel for communication. You may choose personal routes instead which range from formal to informal e.g. face-to-face, phone and video conferencing, emails and Social Media.

Face-to-Face: This communication channel's impact is the most measurable, as you can evaluate whether your message has been interpreted as intended by direct and immediate feedback. Face-to-face medium transmits richness of physical appearance, body language, voice modulation, and allows instant transmission of information with immediate feedback. This is, of course, the most used and useful channel for events like interviews, office meetings, conferences, negotiations, difficult conversations.

Phone and Video Conferencing: The telecom industry has grown by leaps and bounds and now gives borderless service in facilitating business and social interaction too. We take all this for granted but just a decade back, most of the world had to contend with a landline phone and audio-only mobile. And now suddenly, we are abuzz with a host of tele-conferencing and video-conferencing tools and apps like Zoom, Skype, FaceTime and WhatsApp, which are continuously evolving and becoming feature-rich.

The mediating technology makes it possible to connect through Phone, tele-conference, or video-conference and though connected remotely but along with the verbal content you are able to transmit enthusiasm too with options of vocal variety and body language.

Picking up a phone and talking still remains the most effective tool for negotiating an impasse, sharing a thought or proposal, or garnering support for your business idea; and the feedback is in that instant. Tele-conferencing and video-conferencing are proven collaborative tools and highly efficient in delivering outcomes in the interest of time and number of participants.

Email: Over the years, email has evolved from being a text-only media to extending options in the visual field too. With the advent of GIF files, embedded visuals, animated visuals, click and open images ... emails now bring in a rich experience to the receiver.

At the workplace, emails are good to: impart instructions and processes, or send briefs on the changes and structures in an organization, or initiate formal events like interviews, conferences, and training sessions.

And when there's a need to explore someone's position on a certain topic before you start to persuade, email is a good first step.

In the marketing world email has become a favourite tool for marketers. An **email marketing** specialist is a digital marketer that focuses on building email lists, creating emails, and nurturing leads through written communications.

Social Media: The maximum hype today is on Social Media and the most popular platforms are: WhatsApp, Facebook, Instagram, YouTube, and Twitter. Since the content on these can be created by anyone and uploaded on to the social media platform, mostly purposed as a blend of information and entertainment, this is perceived to be the least trusted media. These are free cross-platforms. And being without any entrance barrier, or any verification process to check, Social Media has become a minefield of suspect communication.

However, Social Media is effective for disseminating information. The bonus is that it is instant and has almost no barriers in communication, as long as supported by technological facilitation.

Another interesting thing to note is that nowadays, whether you are you are looking for a date or a job, you are looking at the prospective's social profile. The demographic profile is easy to garner but you are looking for psychographics: attitude, behaviors, reputation, and values of the concerned person or company through the lens of social media. Any hiring process now goes through the wring of social media, whether the candidate has affiliations – religious or political or belongs to any cult – which is undesirable for the company. The personality profile can be drawn from social media like Facebook, Twitter or Instagram, so you need to be careful as to what you publish there!

The Three Ways of Persuasion: Booster Dose

The easiest categorization:

1. Coercion
2. Cooperation
3. Commitment

Coercion, or converting someone by use of force or threat, happens when the target audience feels there's no other option but to surrender or agree. This technique is used in emotional blackmail and psychological manipulation. Persuasion by coercion may also include authority communication like Parent to a child, or Teacher to a student, or Doctor to a patient. Coercion is intended to intimidate the person; it discourages a free two-way communication and results in the intended action, but does not build on goodwill and is not a long-term option.

Persuasion by **Cooperation** is like a family or a team event, where both sides have a buy-in; they negotiate, and come to decided strategy or plan. Importantly, both have vested interests so it is easier to actualize it. However, it does not unleash the full potential of the people engaged; and the team members are more or less complying with the rules set for easier functioning.

Persuasion by **Commitment** is the strongest way of persuading and is practiced by leaders who have been able to groom followers committed to the cause. The members strongly identify with the vision of the captain. Here lies the skill of upholding a sharply defined, shared common goal, and imbibing the followers with enthusiasm for the cause. Each member becomes the cheerleader for the cause.

In the above ways of persuasion, some clear examples can be: Coercion - obey the class monitor or your complaint will go to the teacher. Cooperation - apartment owners requested to provide identity cards for all their staff to the RWA (Residents Welfare Association) so that everybody benefits with better security measures. Commitment - who can be a better example than Gandhiji who made a clarion call for boycott of foreign goods in 1931, won millions to the cause of liberation of India from the British rule, and people enthusiastically joined him in burning foreign goods? That is unadulterated commitment.

At workplace, relatable examples could be: Coercion - coming to office at a set time or there will be salary deduction. Cooperation - executing a plan as per shared timelines for a team implementing a new project. Commitment - being a buddy or accountability partner to a new entrant for problem-solving and celebrating small victories. Your challenge is to raise your persuasion skills through the stages till it reaches commitment.

Neeraj, my friend and an entrepreneur, has founded a business of rent-a-party-dress called *Wrapd,* with a chain of stores in India. She says her objective is more about sustainability than to make money. People buy occasion-wear clothes, wear it just a couple of times, and then it joins the discard pile; while in her vision, people should make a conscious choice to ***rent*** these high-value occasion-wear apparel and conserve resources. Making this choice would be an uptick towards preserving ecology, minimalism and sustainability. Wrapd has a dedicated following who believe in her, her ideals, and are committed customers; her persuasion mission is dedicated to a higher ideal.

We can see that transitioning between the three layers upwards will have maximum benefit and buy-in.

Committed we stand. Together.

The Two Strategies for Persuasion: Understand the Golden Point

Now to make an impactful message, you must:

- Target audience Needs and Motivations
- Chisel your Strategy to address those needs and motivations

Let's take look at Maslow's Hierarchy of Human Needs:

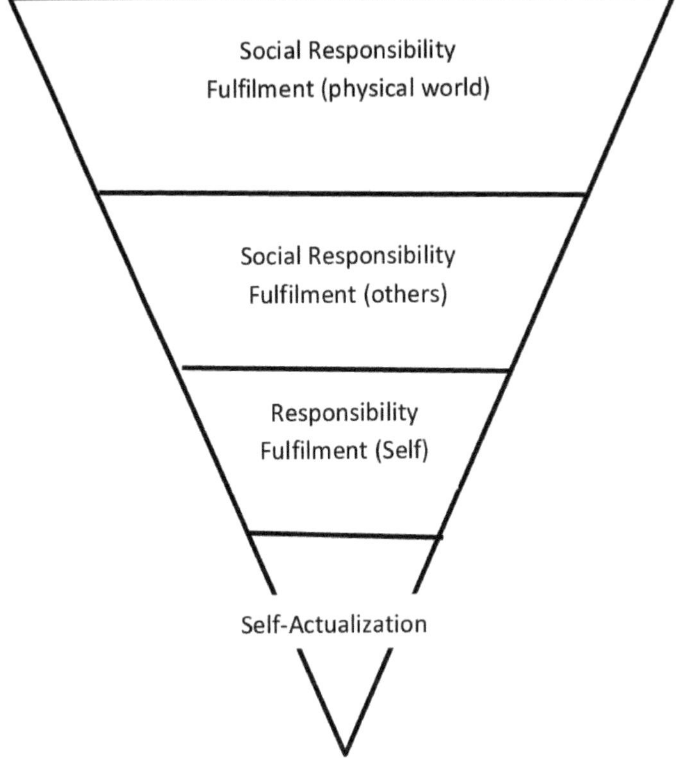

The upside-down figure of Maslow's Hierarchy of Needs

Maslow's hierarchy of needs tells us that as humans, we **communicate** to meet a range of different needs, both physical and social. These include physical needs - for survival, safety and protection, need for belonging, need for self-esteem and need for self-actualization.

As we can see, once the basic needs are met, the human mind is in quest to fulfil self-actualization needs and motivations.

Clearly, it is important for you to understand your listener's need and craft your message and communication strategy accordingly. That is a smart communicator's way of working.

And the cycle is never complete without **Evaluation.**

Hit the Bullseye! Achieve your Goal

Bullseye principle is a definitive guide for excelling in effective communication and aiming to hit the target. Your message, the intent should be clearly defined, and post-communication you should know whether you have achieved it. It could relate to change in attitudes, feelings, beliefs, acceptance, closure or call to action.

You can award yourself the honor of being an Effective Communicator when you have reached your goal.

Preparing to hit the Bullseye:

- Understand the difference between information and persuasion
- Come up with a powerful argument
- Back your arguments with solid research
- Craft your message to be clear, concise, consistent, and credible
- Build Credibility with your audience by displaying first-hand knowledge or experience of something you can backup with facts and figures
- Convey advantages of embracing a situation
- Build authority with awards, achievements, qualifications, associations

- Build Bonds with your Audience
- Work on increased Social Influence: Engage and encourage your audience to cheer for your idea

While shooting the arrow:

- Choose the right time and the right channel of communication
- Understand and use body language and apt non-verbal cues
- Watch what you say! Be the stimulus, and not the response

Post shooting the arrow:

- Listen intently, get your feedback; helps avoiding time wasted in repetition and clarification
- Your communication strategy should spell "Success" in the eyes of the receiver
- Persuade, Motivate, Influence: in that sequence

You have achieved Bullseye:

- Won over people to your ideas, way of thinking, and positivity
- You have reaped rewards for being an Effective Communicator
- Envision yourself with all qualities you desire to have, and build it steadily

You are what you communicate.

"Seek first to understand, then to be understood"

~ Stephen Covey

"Stop setting goals. Goals are pure fantasy until you have a specific plan to achieve them"

I love the way I communicate .... effectively and enjoyably!

Credit Affirmations: http://affirmyourlife.blogspot.com/2009/08/communication-affirmations.html

About The Author

Mohita Datta Mohita Datta is an Author, Communication Coach, Public Speaker, and Soft Skills Trainer. As a qualified and certified coach, she has helped countless people transform their professional lives via her workshops, writings, and seminars.

Mohita Datta dedicates all her creative work to her muse - Communications. It is this passion which strings along all her work: written, verbal or presentational.

Her book, "15 Mantras for Effective Communication" is a step-by-step guide to hone communication skills.

Mohita is also winner of Toastmaster's trophies for Public Speaking; she is an articulate anchor, and a consummate storyteller.

She's a Changemaker and joyful learner too, imbibing new teachings with equal vigor.

You can find more about her, and her work in the field of Communication at www.mohitadatta.com

Coming Soon

Insightful, engaging, and learning books on the core skill of Communication: how it impacts your life, shapes your personality, decides the outcome, and can give you happiness.

Books to further strengthen your Communication skills are coming your way soon. 15 Mantras For Effective Communication is the first one in the sequel as we build our way to niche skills like how to sell your ideas, ideas revolution, actionable strategies, acing your interview, negotiation skills.

Connect on:

Instagram.com/mohita_datta

facebook.com/Fifth Chakraa

Twitter/Mohita Datta

www.mohitadatta.com

Attend ongoing workshops and online sessions on Corporate Communication and Critical Communication Skills, write at: mohita.datta@gmail.com

9 798885 551984

Printed by Libri Plureos GmbH in Hamburg,
Germany